Handwriting
Activity Book

for ages 8-9

This CGP book is bursting with fun activities
to build up children's skills and confidence.

It's ideal for extra practice to reinforce what
they're learning in primary school. Enjoy!

 # Handwriting Hints

Here are some tips to help you keep your writing neat:

1. Make sure your writing rests on the line.

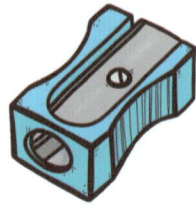

2. Try to keep the spaces between words even.

3. Don't rush. Take your time and concentrate on keeping your writing as neat and tidy as possible.

4. Letters of the same type should be the same size:
   - small letters (like c and o) should all be the same height
   - the tops of tall letters (like k and l) should go up to the same height
   - the tails on letters like g and y should be the same length

5. Remember that a 't' is a bit shorter than tall letters.

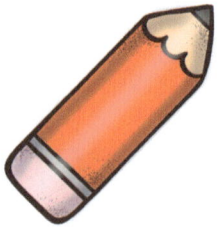

6. Capital letters should be the same height as tall letters.

7. Keep the downstrokes of letters straight and make sure they tilt by the same amount.

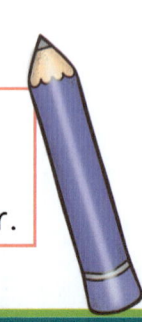

Every school has its own handwriting style. Some schools may form letters and joins differently to how they're written here. Check with the school to see how they write and join each letter.

Contents

Alphabet practice	2
More alphabet practice	4
Capital letters	6
Adverbs	8
Word endings	10
More word endings	12
Puzzle: Find the leader	14
Prepositions	16
Double letters	18
More double letters	20
Rainbow recipe	22
Fairground fun	24
Courageous characters	26
Wizard wandering	28
Answers	30

Published by CGP

Editors:
Andy Cashmore, Helen Clements,
Rachel Craig-McFeely, Alex Fairer

With thanks to Alison Griffin and
Catherine Heygate for the proofreading.

With thanks to Alice Dent
for the copyright research.

ISBN: 978 1 83774 040 6

Printed by Elanders Ltd, Newcastle upon Tyne.
Graphics used on the cover and throughout the book
© Educlips 2023
Cover design concept by emc design ltd.

Text, design, layout and original illustrations
© Coordination Group Publications Ltd. (CGP) 2023
All rights reserved.

Photocopying this book is not permitted, even if you have a CLA licence.
Extra copies are available from CGP with next day delivery • 0800 1712 712 • www.cgpbooks.co.uk

Alphabet practice

How It Works

The words on these pages start with letters from the first half of the alphabet. Work through the questions to get some practice writing these letters.

Remember — your writing should rest on the line.

Now Try These

1. Copy out the words three times on the lines below.

   amber

   brown

   crimson

   dark blue

   emerald

2. Can you copy each of these words out twice?

   fuchsia   gold   hazel   indigo

   jade   khaki   lavender   magenta

3. Now copy out the phrases below.

   amazing artist

   drawing expert

   handmade frame

   fancy gallery

   complex image

   large brush

4. Here are some longer phrases. Can you copy them out on the lines?

   aqua and burgundy   *ivory and mustard*

   canvas for artwork   *her lilac crayon*

An Extra Challenge

Hilda wants to serve snacks for the opening of her art exhibition. Use joined up writing to write a list of foods that Hilda could buy.

Each item should start with one of the first thirteen letters of the alphabet. There should be at least one item for each letter.

Were these pages picture perfect? Tick one of the boxes.

More alphabet practice

How It Works

These pages will help you practise writing letters from the second half of the alphabet.

Watch out for break letters — you don't need to join them to the following letter.

Now Try These

1. Copy out the name of each animal on the lines below.

newt    ostrich

_____   _____

pelican    quokka

_____   _____

rabbit    squirrel

_____   _____

 toucan   unicorn

_____   _____

vixen    walrus

_____   _____

yak   zebra

 _____   _____

4

2. Have a go at copying the phrases below.

thrilling safari *yellow weasel*

naughty penguin *young snake*

whale spotting *velvety raccoon*

3. Now can you copy out these longer phrases?

their quiet spider

our upbeat ocelot

the excited zookeeper

An Extra Challenge

Ewan is getting some new animals at his zoo. He's created signs for the new animals, but the letters are scrambled up.

First unscramble the words and rewrite them using joined up writing. Then write the signs in alphabetical order.

nihor getir otcupos oprart harks

Did you have a wild time on these pages? Tick a box.

Capital letters

How It Works

Proper nouns are names for particular people, places or things. They always start with a capital letter.

Capital letters never join to other letters.

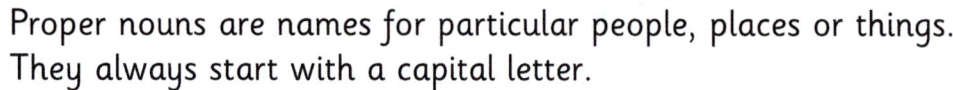

Aaron   Italy   Wednesday

Now Try These

1. Copy out each day of the week three times on the lines below.

Monday _____

Thursday _____

Friday _____

Sunday _____

2. Copy the phrases below.

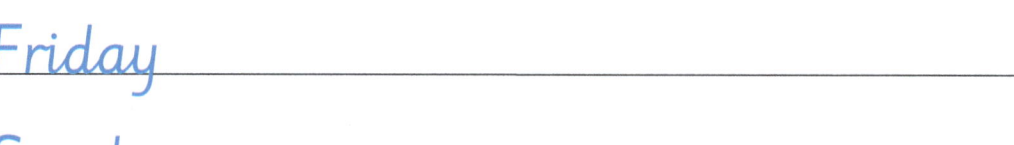 

Easter egg _____   Burns Night _____

Diwali festival _____   Hanukkah _____

Shrove Tuesday _____   St Patrick's Day _____

3. Can you copy out the phrases to show what's happening in the picture?

dark, spooky Halloween

Isla and Ling's pumpkin

Karl's silly costume

chilly English woods

4. Copy out the sentences below.

Valentine's Day is in February.

His family are celebrating Chinese New Year.

Zara can't wait for Christmas Day.

An Extra Challenge

Jamal goes ice-skating once a month and wants to choose a different friend to go with him each time. To help him, write all the months of the year in order. Next to each month, write down the name of one of his friends on the right.

Use capital letters and joined up writing.

Ayesha	Nanako
Colin	Peter
Fabio	Raheem
Grace	Tristan
Imran	Valerie
Laura	Wayne

Did you have a fun time?
Tick a box to show how you did.

Adverbs

How It Works

Adverbs are words that describe verbs. They can tell you how, when and how often the verb is done. Adverbs often end with -ly.

badly   **soon**   **rarely**

Use these pages to help you practise writing adverbs clearly.

Now Try These

1. Can you copy out all of the adverbs on the lines below?

   happily   *skilfully*   *often*

   easily   *poorly*   *boldly*

   angrily   *later*   *clearly*

2. Have a go at copying the phrases below.

   always first   *jog slowly*   *leap boldly*

   normally fast   *training hard*

3. Now copy these longer phrases.

   he dives expertly

   quietly watches them

   swims very quickly

   bravely jumps in

   kicks along strongly

4. Copy the sentences below, replacing the whistles with the missing -ly endings.

   The team proud🎽 stepped onto the pitch.

   She nervous🎽 took the final penalty.

   The crowd usual🎽 cheered loud🎽.

An Extra Challenge

Jenna has written a report about a race, but in her excitement she hasn't added any spaces or full stops. Rewrite the sentences with the right spacing and full stops.

Justinsprintedswiftlyintothelead

Thenheclumsilytrippedandsadlylost

Do you feel like a winner after these pages? Tick a box.

Word endings

How It Works

Some word endings are used a lot, such as -sure, -ture and -gue. It's important to know how to write these clearly.

*lei*sure   *ma*ture   *lea*gue

Now Try These

1. Copy out each of these word endings four times.

   sure

   ture

   gue

2. Have a go at copying the words below.

   dialogue   insure   furniture   pleasure

3. Now try copying these phrases.

   don't argue   ensure safety   puncture fixed

   fatigue from adventure   apply pressure

   must treasure nature

4. Can you copy out each of the sentences below?

My colleague drew a picture of a monkey.

The rogue explorer wants to capture leopards.

My knowledge of their culture is vague.

I'm unsure about the future of the expedition.

The enclosure will feature many animals.

An Extra Challenge

Miguel has found the secret diary of an ancient explorer, but some of the words are written backwards. Rewrite the passage with the words the right way around. Make sure you use joined up writing.

My journey went poorly. There
was a lot of erutsiom in the air
and I wasn't able to erusaem
the eugnot of the rare erutaerc.

Did you find exploring these pages easy? Tick a box.

More word endings

How It Works

Some other common word endings are -tion, -sion and -cian.
You need to be confident about writing these word endings as well.

*ac**tion** occa**sion** politi**cian***

Now Try These

1. Can you copy out these word endings four times?

   tion

   sion

   cian

2. Copy these words on the lines below.

   physician   session   portion   version

3. Have a go at copying these phrases.

   the scientist's mission

   research the erosion

   very tricky question

   solve the equation

   the magician's lab

4. Copy out the sentences below.

The mathematician did some revision.

The technician created an explosion.

The chemicals caused a reaction.

Martin loves addition and division.

Do not mention the television experiment.

An Extra Challenge

Serena has invented a robot that writes down everything she says, but it keeps scrambling some words. Unscramble the words in red and rewrite the passage.

I made the dceosini to help a mainusic with my latest ienvntoin. It's a soinolut to his problems with bad vniiso.

All of the words that need unscrambling end with -sion, -tion or -cian.

How was experimenting with these pages? Tick a box.

Find the leader

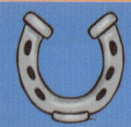

Leah wants to join a group of cowboys and cowgirls called the Writing Rangers, but first she needs to find their leader. Can you help her? Complete the tasks and use the clues to figure out which numbered person is the leader.

1. Rewrite this sentence so that it uses capital letters correctly.

   Our Leader, Sam, Hates Pink Hats.

2. For each box, rearrange the words to form a sentence and write it out. Only the sentence with an adverb is true.

   | enjoy   large   They being   near   rocks |

   | dislike   strongly They large   rocks |

3. Some of the words in the sentence below are missing double letters. Rewrite the sentence, adding the double letters.

   Kitens make the leader sneze, so the leader canot stand next to them.

14

4. Rewrite this passage with the right spacing.

Theleaderisunsureaboutcowsandhas madethedecisiontostayawayfromthem.

___

5. Unscramble the words in red and rewrite the passage.

The leader sirde a ealp horse. They also feel nervous desebi water, so they vadio it.

___

Which person is the leader?
Write the number as a word below.

___

Prepositions

How It Works

Prepositions tell you where, when or why things happen.

under   after   due to

Some prepositions are made up of more than one word.

Now Try These

1. Try copying out these prepositions.

   into   _across_

   from   _beside_

   within   _around_

   past   _prior to_

2. Now copy these phrases containing prepositions.

   opposite his map   _beyond the beach_

   during their journey   _among the pirates_

   through the waves   _since last week_

3. Circle the preposition in each sentence. Then copy each sentence onto the line.

The parrot is always awake before me.

We can't depart because of the storm.

The gigantic cannons are hidden below deck.

The white sails are high above the ship.

You must walk along the plank.

An Extra Challenge

Captain Purplehat wrote down how to get to her hidden treasure, but some of the words have been washed away. Rewrite the instructions, filling in the gaps with the correct words from the list on the right. You should use joined up writing.

Sail your ship ✺ Skull Island.
Find the cave ✺ the tree with blue leaves.
Follow the signs ✺ the narrow tunnel.
Then look for the chest ✺ two statues.
Knock loudly ✺ the chest three times.

between
to
near
on
through

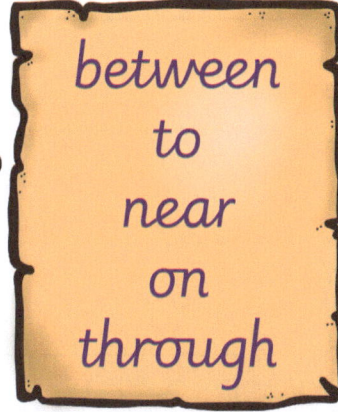

Did yarr sail through these pages? Tick a box.

Double letters

How It Works

Double letters appear in words quite a lot — tt, ff, ee and rr are some of them. You'll get plenty of practice writing these double letters on the next two pages.

spotted   handcuff   flee   sorry

Now Try These

1. Have a go at copying these pairs of letters four times.

   tt _____   ff _____

   ee _____   rr _____

2. Next, copy the words on the lines below.

   attack   _staff_   _career_   _irritate_

   _____   _____   _____   _____

3. Can you copy these phrases?

   the speeding traffic

   he scattered litter

   agreed to surrender

   plotting a crime

   she preferred justice

4. Now copy out the sentences below.

Someone sprayed graffiti on the cottage.

She spotted the expensive mirror being stolen.

The three policemen often disagreed.

The offender enjoys knitting scarves.

An officer arrested a sneaky suspect.

An Extra Challenge

Detective Gav has accidentally missed out letters in his report of an unusual crime. Rewrite the sentences below, adding the right letters to the words in red.

This terrible crime is dificult to solve. At the wekend, boxes of chese and letuce went missing from a shop. The shopkeper thinks a bufalo is responsible. This must be incorect.

Don't forget to use neat, joined up writing.

Were you happy working this case? Tick a box.

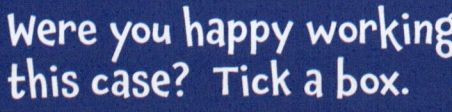    

19

More double letters

How It Works

It's time to practise some more double letters — dd, mm, nn and ll. These will crop up a fair bit, so you should get used to writing them.

saddle command sunny hall

Now Try These

1. Copy each pair of letters four times.

   dd   mm

   nn   ll

2. Can you copy these words on the lines below?

   paddock   summer   banner   villain

3. Have a go at copying these phrases.

   my stunning crown   the prince's wedding

   the queen's hammock   in our ballroom

   his annoying horse

4. Now copy these sentences out neatly on the lines below.

The cunning dragon gave them a riddle.

Fix the castle door with your hammer.

My whole village rebelled against the queen.

Prince Hiro is winning the swimming race.

The king wants you to fetch his ladder.

An Extra Challenge

Fran and Dan have written about a jousting tournament, but they haven't added any spaces or full stops. Rewrite the sentences with the right spacing and full stops.

FransummonedtheexcellentriderHis facewashiddenandhishorsewas runningstronglyDanannouncedthe secondriderwhoshudderedfearfully

Did you rule these pages? Tick a box to show how you got on.

Rainbow recipe

How It Works

You've made some great progress with your handwriting skills.

Now it's time to practise longer pieces of writing with this recipe.

Now Try These

1. Start by writing the first sentences of the recipe on the lines below.

   Gather food colouring for each cake layer.

   Mix eggs, butter and sugar together.

2. Now have a go at writing these pairs of sentences.

   Gently sieve the flour into the mixture.
   Then divide equally into seven bowls.

   Add a splash of food colouring to each bowl.
   Use a different colour for every bowl.

3. Copy out the passage below to complete the recipe.

Pour each mixture into a separate tin and bake. Leave to cool, then add icing between each layer. Make sure you order your layers to follow the colours of the rainbow.

An Extra Challenge

Chef Guro has created a brilliant new recipe, but she's written the instructions in the wrong order. Rewrite the passage below with the instructions in the correct order. Make sure you use your neatest joined up handwriting.

Then mix the sauce thoroughly and add it to the mince. Scoop the mixture into the wraps and cook for ten minutes. After adding the sauce, sprinkle in some cheese and stir. Firstly, heat the mince in a pan.

Was that an appetising pair of pages? Tick a box.

Fairground fun

How It Works

Here's some more practice at writing longer passages.

This time, you'll be writing lines from rhyming poems.

Now Try These

1. Copy the opening lines of this poem.

    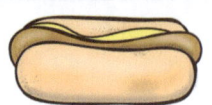

    I'm excited to visit the fairground,
    Where the lively rides go round and round.

2. Can you copy these lines from the next verse?

    First we ride the bumper cars,
    Swerving to avoid being hit.
    Next we hold on tight to the bars,
    As the pirate ship nearly flips.

3. Finish off the poem by copying the last verse.

The rollercoaster grabs my attention,
I run and claim the front seats with my friend.
The carriage moves, I feel its vibration,
Suddenly we dip and dive through a bend.
We zoom violently in every direction,
Then halt with a jolt when we reach the end.

An Extra Challenge

Here's a poem about a Ferris wheel. Think of one word that could replace the candyfloss at the end of each line so all the lines rhyme. Then write out the poem using joined up writing.

First we go up and then we go
From up high we see the whole of
Everyone smiles, there's not a single

Hint: the missing words all rhyme with crown.

Did you find that thrilling?
Tick a box to show how you did.

Courageous characters

How It Works

Well done on all of your hard work so far. Practice makes perfect though, so it's time to tackle some more questions.

Use your handwriting skills to write out these passages about superheroes as neatly as you can.

Now Try These

1. Copy the passage below about this superhero.

   Lemon Lass is a superhero with unusual powers. She can turn criminals into lemons using her juice squirter, and uses lemon rinds to become bulletproof. She has other powers too, like flying. You can often see her boldly speeding across the sky in her yellow suit.

2. Can you copy out this description of Lemon Lass's foe?

Tornado Tyrant lives in a mansion in the clouds. People worry when they spot his green cape in the sky because it means he's about to cause destruction. He breathes in deeply and then spits out terrifying tornadoes that bring chaos to towns and their citizens.

An Extra Challenge

Write your own description of a superhero. Use the facts below to help you.

Use neat, joined up writing.

- Can turn invisible
- Always wears sunglasses
- Has blue hair
- Lives underground

Did you have a super time with these pages? Tick a box.

Wizard wandering

How It Works

Great job — you're quickly becoming a handwriting expert.

Try the activities on these pages to really test your handwriting skills.

Now Try These

1. Read the directions to the wizard's cave. Then copy them onto the lines on the next page.

Enter the woods through the golden gate at the bottom of Willow Lane. Walk straight ahead until you reach the stone sculpture of a unicorn among the trees.
    Gently stroke the unicorn's mane to reveal a path to the pixie village. Proceed with caution and don't eat the glowing berries. Carefully cross the bridge in the centre of the village and take a left at the purple toadstools. You must now climb Magician's Hill. At the top, you will find a stone circle. Hidden behind the largest stone is the entrance to the wizard's cave.

An Extra Challenge

Winnie the witch has lost her wand. Write a set of directions that follow the red path from Winnie to her wand. Use all of the words in the orange box.

Remember to use neat, joined up writing.

gate	bush
horse	through
trees	turn
cottage	beside

Was that magical? Put a tick in a box to show how you did.

Answers

Here are the answers to the Extra Challenges and the puzzle. All answers should be written in joined up writing.

Pages 2-3 — Alphabet practice

You should have written a list of snacks that start with the first thirteen letters of the alphabet.

Pages 4-5 — More alphabet practice

Unscrambled words: rhino, tiger, octopus, parrot, shark
In alphabetical order: octopus, parrot, rhino, shark, tiger

Pages 6-7 — Capital letters

You should have written the months of the year and the names in the list with capital letters and joined up writing.

Pages 8-9 — Adverbs

Justin sprinted swiftly into the lead. Then he clumsily tripped and sadly lost.

Pages 10-11 — Word endings

My journey went poorly. There was a lot of moisture in the air and I wasn't able to measure the tongue of the rare creature.

Pages 12-13 — More word endings

I made the decision to help a musician with my latest invention. It's a solution to his problems with bad vision.

Pages 14-15 — Find the leader

1. Our leader, Sam, hates pink hats.
2. They enjoy being near large rocks. (false)
   They strongly dislike large rocks. (true — strongly is an adverb)
3. Kittens make the leader sneeze, so the leader cannot stand next to them.
4. The leader is unsure about cows and has made the decision to stay away from them.
5. The leader rides a pale horse. They also feel nervous beside water, so they avoid it.

The leader is person number four.

Pages 16-17 — Prepositions

Sail your ship to Skull Island. Find the cave near the tree with blue leaves. Follow the signs through the narrow tunnel. Then look for the chest between two statues. Knock loudly on the chest three times.

Pages 18-19 — Double letters

This terrible crime is difficult to solve. At the weekend, boxes of cheese and lettuce went missing from a shop. The shopkeeper thinks a buffalo is responsible. This must be incorrect.

Pages 20-21 — More double letters

Fran summoned the excellent rider. His face was hidden and his horse was running strongly. Dan announced the second rider who shuddered fearfully.

Pages 22-23 — Rainbow recipe

Firstly, heat the mince in a pan. Then mix the sauce thoroughly and add it to the mince. After adding the sauce, sprinkle in some cheese and stir. Scoop the mixture into the wraps and cook for ten minutes.

Pages 24-25 — Fairground fun

Any sensible words that rhyme with crown.
E.g. down, town, frown

Pages 26-27 — Courageous characters

You should have written a description of a superhero using the facts given.

Pages 28-29 — Wizard wandering

Any sensible set of directions that use the words in the box and guide Winnie along the red path to her wand.
E.g. Climb over the wooden gate and go forward until you reach the horse. Then turn right and go through the trees. Beside the cottage you'll see a bush. Reach into the bush and grab the wand.